hen

курка
kurka

rooster

півень
piven

chick

курча
kurcha

duckling

каченя
kachenia

turkey

індик
indyk

donkey

віслюк
visliuk

swan

лебідь
lebid

frog

жаба
zhaba

racoon

єнот
ienot

bear

ведмідь
vedmid

squirrel

білка
bilka

fly

муха
mukha

ladybug

божа корівка

bozha korivka

worm

черв'як

cherv'iak

snail

равлик

ravlyk

slug

слимак

slymak

bee

бджола
bdzhola

spider

павук
pavuk

beetle

жук
zhuk

dragonfly

бабка
babka

lion

лев
lev

zebra

зебра
zebra

giraffe

жираф
zhyraf

rhinoceros

носоріг
nosorih

snake

змія

zmiia

mosquito

комар

komar

sea turtle

морська черепаха

morska cherepakha

hippopotamus

бегемот

behemot

alligator

алігатор
alihator

crocodile

крокодил
krokodyl

shark

акула
akula

walrus

морж

morzh

penguin

пінгвін

pinhvin

polar bear

білий ведмідь

bilyi vedmid

seal

тюлень

tiulen

starfish

морська зірка

morska zirka

jellyfish

медуза
meduza

seashells

морські раковини

morski rakovyny

feather

перо
pero

11

eleven

одинадцять

odynadtsiat

12

twelve

дванадцять

dvanadtsiat

13

thirteen

тринадцять

trynadtsiat

14

fourteen

чотирнадцять

chotyrnadtsiat

15

fifteen

п'ятнадцять

p'iatnadtsiat

16

sixteen

шістнадцять

shistnadtsiat

17

seventeen

сімнадцять

simnadtsiat

18

eighteen

вісімнадцять

visimnadtsiat

19

nineteen

дев'ятнадцять
dev'iatnadtsiat

20

twenty

двадцять
dvadtsiat

heart
серце
sertse

oval
овал
oval

arrow
стрілка
strilka

crescent
півмісяць
pivmisiats

curve

крива
kryva

spiral

спіраль
spiral

cross

хрест
khrest

zigzag

зигзаг
zyhzah

rainbow

веселка
veselka

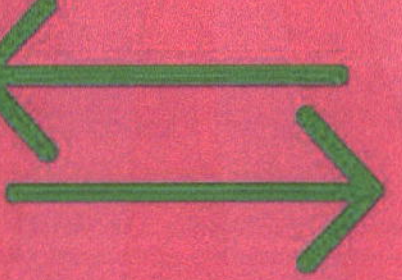

dark colors

темні кольори

temni kolory

light colors

світлі кольори

svitli kolory

dots

крапки
krapky

line

лінія
liniia

short

низький
nyzkyi

tall

високий
vysokyi

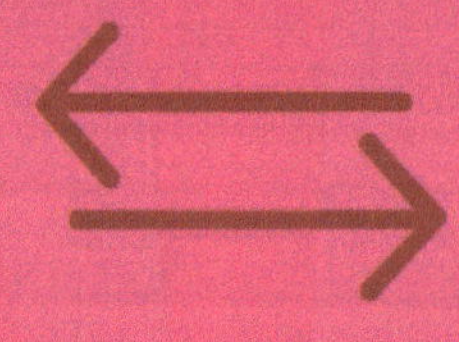

a little

трохи
trokhy

a lot

багато
bahato

full

повний
povnyi

empty

пустий
pustyi

curly hair

кучеряве волосся

kucheriave volossia

straight hair

пряме волосся

priame volossia

accept

приймати

pryimaty

refuse

відмовлятися

vidmovliatysia

identical
однаковий
odnakovyi

different
відмінний
vidminnyi

dry
сухий
sukhyi

wet
мокрий
mokryi

toys

іграшки

ihrashky

blocks

кубики

kubyky

ball

м'яч

m'iach

robots

роботи

roboty

tongue

язик
iazyk

nose

ніс
nis

hair

волосся
volossia

moustache

вуса
vusa

fingers

пальці
paltsi

arm

передпліччя
peredplichchia

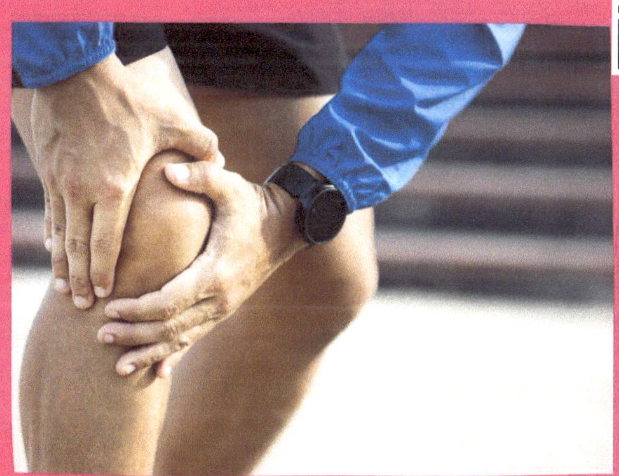

knee

коліно
kolino

elbow

лікоть
likot

smile

посміхатися

posmikhatysia

kiss

поцілунок

potsilunok

cry

плакати

plakaty

pain

біль

bil

body

тіло
tilo

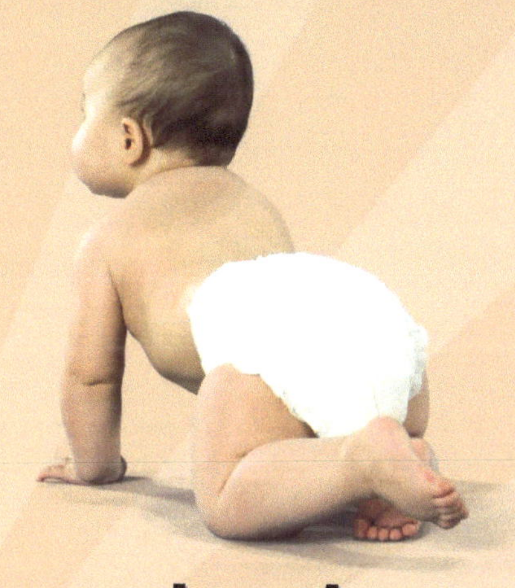

back

спина
spyna

pacifier

соска
soska

high chair

стільчик для годування
stilchyk dlia hoduvannia

soap

мило

mylo

toothbrush

зубна щітка

zubna shchitka

towel

рушник

rushnyk

potty

дитячий горщик

dytiachyi horshchyk

ring

каблучка
kabluchka

bracelet

браслет
braslet

necklace

намисто
namysto

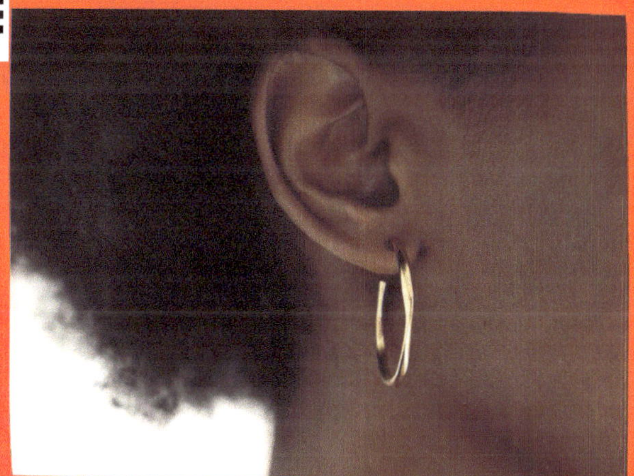

earring

сережка
serezhka

chocolate

шоколад
shokolad

popcorn

попкорн
popkorn

jam

варення
varennia

toast

тост
tost

honey

мед
med

butter

масло
maslo

bread

хліб
khlib

ice cream

морозиво
morozyvo

semolina

манна крупа

manna krupa

rice

рис

rys

pasta

паста

pasta

soup

суп

sup

milk

молоко
moloko

water

вода
voda

juice

сік
sik

kiwi

ківі
kivi

raspberry

малина
malyna

grapefruit

грейпфрут
hreipfrut

melon

диня
dynia

plum

слива
slyva

apricot

абрикос
abrykos

pomegranate

гранат
hranat

fig

інжир
inzhyr

blueberry

чорниця
chornytsia

cranberry

журавлина
zhuravlyna

persimmon

хурма
khurma

lychee

лічі
lichi

fruits

фрукти
frukty

vegetables

овочі
ovochi

avocado

авокадо
avokado

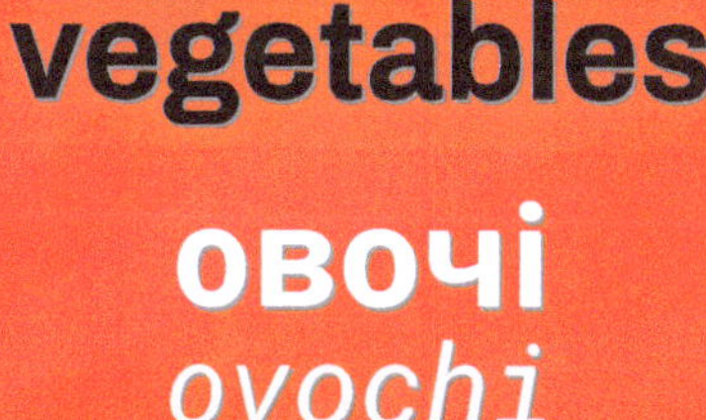

green bean

стручкова квасоля
struchkova kvasolia

broccoli

броколі
brokoli

eggplant

баклажан
baklazhan

peas

горошинки
horoshynky

bell pepper

болгарський перець
bolharskyi perets

beet

буряк
buriak

lettuce

салат-латук
salat-latuk

endive

цикорій салатний
tsykorii salatnyi

artichoke

артишок
artyshok

leek

цибуля-порей

tsybulia-porei

onion

цибуля

tsybulia

garlic

часник

chasnyk

ginger

імбир

imbyr

walnuts

волоські горіхи

voloski horikhy

almond

мигдаль

myhdal

pistachio

фісташки

fistashky

cashew

кеш'ю

kesh'iu